QUIZZES FOR COUPLES

FUN QUESTIONS TO COMPLETE TOGETHER AND STRENGTHEN YOUR RELATIONSHIP

ASHLEY AND MARCUS KUSI

Join Our Community

To receive updates about future books, our monthly inspirational newsletter for couples, workshops, and courses, visit the website below and join our book fan community today.

www.ourpeacefulfamily.com/bookfan

Dedication

To couples committed to making their relationships the best they can be.

Contents

Introduction

Have you ever been asked something about your partner that you couldn't answer right away? Well, we've been there too. And it's an interesting situation to be in because there's always something new to learn about the one you love.

That's why we created *Quizzes for Couples*, a fun quiz book to help you and your partner *truly* know each other. Completing the quizzes together will provide you with many opportunities to have engaging conversations and discover new things about each other.

First, you will find questions designed as multiple-choice, yes/no, and short-answer quizzes about your partner and relationship. Topics covered include personality traits, history, goals, friends and family, communication, likes and dislikes, hobbies, a relationship checkup, sex, romance, intimacy, and more.

The questions are grouped into twelve quizzes so you can complete a section each week, or as often as you'd like. We've also included some exciting rewards to try for your quiz results.

Lastly, complete this quiz book with your partner, because it's a fun thing to do together that helps you connect and strengthen your relationship.

Now, turn the page to see how best to use this activity book for couples.

How to Use This Book

It's as easy as one, two, three!

First, decide who will be Partner A and who will be Partner B for the duration of the book.

Partner A: _____

Partner B: _____

Second, go through each quiz section, independently answering the questions. Feel free to take a guess if you don't know an answer. (Don't peek!)

Third, compare your partner's answers with how you really feel about each answer to see just how accurate they are.

Now, get a pen or pencil out, and get started!

Quiz 1
When You Know, You Know

*(Partner **A**: It's your turn to answer.)*

1. What are your partner's three best personality traits?

a. _____ b. _____ c. _____

2. Name one of the stresses your partner is facing right now:

_____

3. What is one thing your partner is most proud of?

_____

4. When was the last time your partner cried?

_____

5. What does your partner normally do in their free time?

_____

6. How does your partner handle stress?

_____

_____

_____

7. If your partner has been warned to not tell a secret, will they tell you?

     Yes   No   Maybe

8. Which skills of yours would your partner like you to teach them?

_____

9. What is your partner's most unique talent?

_____

10. What is your partner's most valued possession?

_____

11. One family tradition your partner loves is . . .

_____

12. Do you think your partner feels loved, respected, and appreciated by you?

     Yes   No   Maybe

13. Is your partner afraid you will leave them?

    Yes   No   Maybe

14. Does your partner often feel criticized by you?

    Yes   No   Maybe

15. What is one way you can make your partner smile when they are upset about something?

_____

_____

_____

16. What's an item on their wish list?

_____

17. Is your partner allergic to anything?

    Yes   No

If yes, what are they are allergic to?

_____

Awesome, you just finished yours. Now, turn the page for your partner to complete their questions.

When You Know, You Know

1. What are your partner's three best personality traits?

a. _____ b. _____ c. _____

2. Name one of the stresses your partner is facing right now:

_____

3. What is one thing your partner is most proud of?

_____

4. When was the last time your partner cried?

_____

5. What does your partner normally do in their free time?

_____

6. How does your partner handle stress?

_____

_____

_____

7. If your partner has been warned to not tell a secret, will they tell you?

     Yes   No   Maybe

8. Which skills of yours would your partner like you to teach them?

_____

9. What is your partner's most unique talent?

_____

10. What is your partner's most valued possession?

_____

11. One family tradition your partner loves is . . .

_____

12. Do you think your partner feels loved, respected, and appreciated by you?

     Yes   No   Maybe

13. Is your partner afraid you will leave them?

     Yes   No   Maybe

14. Does your partner often feel criticized by you?

     Yes   No   Maybe

15. What is one way you can make your partner smile when they are upset about something?

_____

_____

_____

16. What's an item on their wish list?

_____

17. Is your partner allergic to anything?

     Yes   No

If yes, what are they are allergic to?

_____

You are done with yours. Turn the page to review your quiz results together.

Review Your Results

Discuss both of your answers and review how you and your partner view things differently.

Use this review as a chance to revisit any question(s) you would like to have a deeper conversation about with your partner.

Quiz Results for this Section

What's the total number of questions you got correct about your partner?

Partner A: _____

Partner B: _____

The partner with the highest score gets to pick the next movie or show you watch together.

If it's a tie, give each other an endearing hug and a passionate kiss. Then, say "I love you."

Quiz 2
Think About It

(Partner A: It's your turn to answer.)

1. Does your partner believe in soul mates?

      Yes   No

2. What are some of the little things that make your partner happy?

_____

_____

_____

3. When do you think your partner first fell in love with you?

_____

_____

_____

4. Which part of your body does your partner love most?

_____

5. Which of your outfits does your partner love to see you in?

_____

6. Does your partner have any birthmarks?

     Yes   No

If yes, where? _____

7. Which of the below would make your partner feel most loved?

     a. Weekly dates   b. Public displays of affection   c. Compliments

     d. Gifts.   e. Love notes   f. Quality time

8. Your partner's idea of a perfect date would be . . .

_____

_____

_____

9. Your partner's ability to _____ is extraordinary.

10. What is your partner's blood type?

_____

11. Does your partner believe in life after death?

    Yes   No

12. Which creature does your partner fear the most?

    a. Snakes   b. Spider   c. Scorpion

    d. Bears   e. Wolves   f. Other: _____

13. Would your partner say you're romantic enough?

    Yes   No

14. Does your partner agree that you both complement each other?

    Yes   No

15. Does your partner love spending time with you?

    Yes   No

16. Does your partner put your needs above their wants?

    a. Always   b. Not really   c. Most of the time

Awesome, you just finished yours. Now, turn the page for your partner to complete theirs.

Think About It

1. Does your partner believe in soul mates?

     Yes   No

2. What are some of the little things that make your partner happy?

_____

_____

_____

3. When do you think your partner first fell in love with you?

_____

_____

_____

4. Which part of your body does your partner love most?

_____

5. Which of your outfits does your partner love to see you in?

_____

6. Does your partner have any birthmarks?

     Yes   No

If yes, where? _____

7. Which of the below would make your partner feel most loved?

    a. Weekly dates   b. Public displays of affection   c. Compliments

    d. Gifts.   e. Love notes   f. Quality time

8. Your partner's idea of a perfect date would be . . .

_____

_____

_____

9. Your partner's ability to _____ is extraordinary.

10. What is your partner's blood type?

_____

11. Does your partner believe in life after death?

    Yes   No

12. Which creature does your partner fear the most?

    a. Snakes   b. Spider   c. Scorpion

    d. Bears   e. Wolves   f. Other: _____

13. Would your partner say you're romantic enough?

    Yes   No

14. Does your partner agree that you both complement each other?

    Yes   No

15. Does your partner love spending time with you?

    Yes   No

16. Does your partner put your needs above their wants?

    a. Always   b. Not really   c. Most of the time

You are done with yours. Turn the page to review your quiz results together.

Review Your Results

Discuss both of your answers and review how you and your partner view things differently.

Use this review as a chance to revisit any question(s) you would like to have a deeper conversation about with your partner.

Quiz Results for this Section

What's the total number of questions you got correct about your partner?

Partner A: _____

Partner B: _____

The partner with the highest score gets to pick a local event or concert to attend together.

If it's a tie, make a list of five things you appreciate about each other.

Quiz 3
Let's Talk About It

(Partner A: It's your turn to answer.)

1. What are three things your partner loves talking about with you?

   a. _____ b. _____ c. _____

2. What three things does your partner like most about you?

   a. _____ b. _____ c. _____

3. One of your partner's biggest pet peeves is . . .

   _____

4. What makes your partner nervous?

   _____

5. What is one thing they hate?

   _____

6. What is one thing they love?

_____

7. What is your partner's most common reaction during a heated argument?

_____

_____

_____

8. When shouldn't you talk to your partner?

_____

9. What would your partner say is the best thing about your relationship?

_____

10. What's one thing your partner would love to learn from an expert?

_____

11. What genre does your partner love to read or, if they don't read, watch on television?

_____

12. How would your partner describe you in one word?

_____

13. What is one subject they find difficult talking to you about?

_____

14. Do you believe your partner shares all their secrets with you?

     Yes   No

15. Would your partner agree to the statement that you both resolve your conflicts effectively?

     Yes   No

16. Does your partner completely trust you?

     Yes   No

17. Does your partner feel heard and completely understood by you?

     Yes   No   Maybe

18. Excluding sex, what is one thing your partner always loves doing with you?

_____

Awesome, you just finished yours. Now, turn the page for your partner to complete theirs.

Let's Talk About It

*(Partner **B**: It's your turn to answer.)*

1. What are three things your partner loves talking about with you?

a. _____ b. _____ c. _____

2. What three things does your partner like most about you?

a. _____ b. _____ c. _____

3. One of your partner's biggest pet peeves is . . .

_____

4. What makes your partner nervous?

_____

5. What is one thing they hate?

_____

6. What is one thing they love?

_____

7. What is your partner's most common reaction during a heated argument?

_____

_____

_____

8. When shouldn't you talk to your partner?

_____

9. What would your partner say is the best thing about your relationship?

_____

10. What's one thing your partner would love to learn from an expert?

_____

11. What genre does your partner love to read or, if they don't read, watch on television?

_____

12. How would your partner describe you in one word?

_____

13. What is one subject they find difficult talking to you about?

_____

14. Do you believe your partner shares all their secrets with you?

    Yes   No

15. Would your partner agree to the statement that you both resolve your conflicts effectively?

    Yes   No

16. Does your partner completely trust you?

    Yes   No

17. Does your partner feel heard and completely understood by you?

    Yes   No   Maybe

18. Excluding sex, what is one thing your partner always loves doing with you?

_____

You are done with yours. Turn the page to review your quiz results together.

Review Your Results

Discuss both of your answers and review how you and your partner view things differently.

Use this review as a chance to revisit any question(s) you would like to have a deeper conversation about with your partner.

Quiz Results for this Section

What's the total number of questions you got correct about your partner?

Partner A: _____

Partner B: _____

The partner with the highest score gets to have their car cleaned out by the partner with the lowest score.

If it's a tie, snuggle and cuddle together for at least twenty minutes.

Quiz 4
Friends and Family

*(Partner **A**: It's your turn to answer.)*

1. Who has been a strong positive influence on your partner's personal development?

_____

2. Which friend of yours does your partner trust the most?

_____

3. Who is your partner's best friend?

_____

4. Does your partner want their parent(s) to live with you when they get older?

     Yes   No

5. What is the relationship between your partner and your parent(s) like?

     a. Non-existent   b. They tolerate each other

     c. Good   d. Amazing

6. Which couple would your partner choose to go on a double date with?

_____

7. Which of your relatives does your partner like the most?

_____

8. Does your partner get along with your friends?

      a. Yes   b. Usually   c. Not really

9. Who would your partner donate a kidney to? (Circle all that apply)

      a. You   b. A sibling   c. A friend

      d. A relative   e. A stranger in need   f. Nobody

10. Out of your circle of friends, who does your partner think is the happiest in their relationship?

_____

11. What is something about parenting you can both agree on?

_____

12. Other than you, who would your partner turn to for advice if you were having issues in your relationship?

_____

13. One positive trait your partner got from their parent(s) is . . .

_____

Awesome, you just finished yours. Now, turn the page for your partner to complete theirs.

Friends and Family

*(Partner **B**: It's your turn to answer.)*

1. Who has been a strong positive influence on your partner's personal development?

_____

2. Which friend of yours does your partner trust the most?

_____

3. Who is your partner's best friend?

_____

4. Does your partner want their parent(s) to live with you when they get older?

     Yes   No

5. What is the relationship between your partner and your parent(s) like?

     a. Non-existent   b. They tolerate each other

     c. Good   d. Amazing

6. Which couple would your partner choose to go on a double date with?

_____

7. Which of your relatives does your partner like the most?

_____

8. Does your partner get along with your friends?

    a. Yes   b. Usually   c. Not really

9. Who would your partner donate a kidney to? (Circle all that apply)

    a. You   b. A sibling   c. A friend

    d. A relative   e. A stranger in need   f. Nobody

10. Out of your circle of friends, who does your partner think is the happiest in their relationship?

_____

11. What is something about parenting you can both agree on?

_____

12. Other than you, who would your partner turn to for advice if you were having issues in your relationship?

_____

13. One positive trait your partner got from their parent(s) is . . .

_____

You are done with yours. Turn the page to review your quiz results together.

Review Your Results

Discuss both of your answers and review how you and your partner view things differently.

Use this review as a chance to revisit any question(s) you would like to have a deeper conversation about with your partner.

Quiz Results for this Section

What's the total number of questions you got correct about your partner?

Partner A: _____

Partner B: _____

The partner with the highest score gets to receive a list of ten things their partner (with the lowest score) is most grateful for and loves about them.

If it's a tie, plan a visit to your closest friends and/or family.

Quiz 5
How Well Do You Really Know Each Other?

*(Partner **A**: It's your turn to answer.)*

1. What is your partner's least favorite housework task?

    a. Dishes   b. Laundry

    c. Bathrooms   d. Tidying up the house

2. What is one of your partner's favorite smells?

_____

3. What is their favorite season?

    a. Fall   b. Spring

    c. Summer   d. Winter

4. What are their hidden talents?

_____

5. What are your partner's top three priorities or goals?

a. _____ b. _____ c. _____

6. What is their favorite animal/pet?

_____

7. What's your partner's love language?

    a. Words of affirmation   b. Acts of service   c. Receiving

    d. Gifts   e. Quality time   f. Physical touch

(If you don't know it, just pick the most appropriate one, then after you finish this section, visit www.ourpeacefulfamily.com/5LLquiz to take the quiz for free.)

8. What is the first thing your partner would do if they won the lottery?

_____

9. Which is their zodiac sign?

     a. Aries   b. Leo   c. Cancer

     d. Pisces   e. Scorpio   f. Taurus

     g. Sagittarius   h. Gemini   i. Virgo

     j. Libra   k. Capricorn   l. Aquarius

10. Which historical figure would your partner love to have a chat with?

_____

11. What is the first thing your partner does after waking in the morning?

_____

12. What is the last thing your partner does before going to bed each night?

_____

13. Who is one of their favorite authors?

_____

14. What are your partner's favorite meals?

_____

15. Which foods does your partner hate?

_____

16. What helps your partner to fall asleep?

_____

17. Does your partner believe in ghosts?

     Yes   No

18. Which holiday gets your partner more excited?

    a. Christmas   b. Birthdays   c. Our anniversary

    d. Thanksgiving/Harvest   e. Halloween   f. Other: _____

19. Your partner prefers . . .

     a. Paperbacks   b. eBooks

     c. Audiobooks   d. None

20. Does your partner tend to run . . .

     a. Late   b. Early   c. On time

21. What are your partner's favorite hobbies?

_____

_____

_____

22. What is one thing in your household your partner would like to replace?

_____

23. What TV show can't your partner do without?

_____

24. If your partner had to move out of the country, where would they go?

_____

25. What is their favorite flower?

_____

26. Your partner's favorite charity or cause to support is . . .

_____

27. What's their favorite romantic gesture?

_____

Awesome, you just finished yours. Now, turn the page for your partner to complete theirs.

How Well Do you Really Know Each Other?

*(Partner **B**: It's your turn to answer.)*

1. What is your partner's least favorite housework task?

    a. Dishes   b. Laundry

    c. Bathrooms   d. Tidying up the house

2. What is one of your partner's favorite smells?

_____

3. What is their favorite season?

    a. Fall   b. Spring

    c. Summer   d. Winter

4. What are their hidden talents?

_____

5. What are your partner's top three priorities or goals?

a. _____ b. _____ c. _____

6. What is their favorite animal/pet?

_____

7. What's your partner's love language?

a. Words of affirmation   b. Acts of service   c. Receiving

d. Gifts   e. Quality time   f. Physical touch

(If you don't know it, just pick the most appropriate one, then after you finish this section, visit www.ourpeacefulfamily.com/5LLquiz to take the quiz for free.)

8. What is the first thing your partner would do if they won the lottery?

_____

9. Which is their zodiac sign?

a. Aries   b. Leo   c. Cancer

d. Pisces   e. Scorpio   f. Taurus

g. Sagittarius   h. Gemini   i. Virgo

j. Libra   k. Capricorn   l. Aquarius

10. Which historical figure would your partner love to have a chat with?

_____

11. What is the first thing your partner does after waking in the morning?

_____

12. What is the last thing your partner does before going to bed each night?

_____

13. Who is one of their favorite authors?

_____

14. What are your partner's favorite meals?

_____

15. Which foods does your partner hate?

_____

16. What helps your partner to fall asleep?

_____

17. Does your partner believe in ghosts?

     Yes   No

18. Which holiday gets your partner more excited?

    a. Christmas   b. Birthdays   c. Our anniversary

    d. Thanksgiving/Harvest   e. Halloween   f. Other: _____

19. Your partner prefers . . .

      a. Paperbacks   b. eBooks

      c. Audiobooks   d. None

20. Does your partner tend to run . . .

      a. Late   b. Early   c. On time

21. What are your partner's favorite hobbies?

_____

_____

_____

22. What is one thing in your household your partner would like to replace?

_____

23. What TV show can't your partner do without?

_____

24. If your partner had to move out of the country, where would they go?

_____

25. What is their favorite flower?

_____

26. Your partner's favorite charity or cause to support is . . .

_____

27. What's their favorite romantic gesture?

_____

You are done with yours. Turn the page to review your quiz results together.

Review Your Results

Discuss both of your answers and review how you and your partner view things differently.

Use this review as a chance to revisit any question(s) you would like to have a deeper conversation about with your partner.

Quiz Results for this Section

What's the total number of questions you got correct about your partner?

Partner A: _____

Partner B: _____

The partner with the highest score gets to get out of a chore they would usually have done this month, because the partner with the lowest score will complete the task.

If it's a tie, create a bucket list together.

Quiz 6
Looking Back

(Partner A: It's your turn to answer.)

1. When your partner was a child, what did they want to be when they grew up?

_____

2. Where was your partner born?

_____

3. What countries have they been to?

_____

4. What was their first job?

_____

5. What's one fad they fell victim to?

_____

6. What are the best three experiences of their life?

a. _____ b. _____ c. _____

7. If your partner could go back in time, what would they change?

_____

8. Has your partner ever broken the law (aside from traffic violations)?

Yes   No

9. What is the weirdest experience of your partner's life?

_____

_____

_____

10. When has your partner been most scared?

_____

_____

_____

11. How many times did your partner move houses before the age of eighteen?

_____

12. What's your partner's favorite date with you?

_____

_____

_____

13. When was the first time your partner flew on a plane?

_____

14. At what age did your partner leave the home they grew up in?

_____

15. My partner's worst job ever was . . .

_____

16. How old was your partner when they first voted?

_____

17. Has your partner ever been fired from a job?

    Yes   No

18. Has your partner ever won a contest before?

    Yes   No

If yes, what was the prize?

_____

19. What was your partner's first car?

_____

20. Which languages are your partner fluent in?

_____

21. What was your partner's first impression of you?

_____

_____

_____

22. Your partner's favorite memory with you is . . .

_____

_____

_____

Awesome, you just finished yours. Now, turn the page for your partner to complete theirs.

Looking Back

(Partner **B**: It's your turn to answer.)

1. When your partner was a child, what did they want to be when they grew up?

_____

2. Where was your partner born?

_____

3. What countries have they been to?

_____

4. What was their first job?

_____

5. What's one fad they fell victim to?

_____

6. What are the best three experiences of their life?

a. _____ b. _____ c. _____

7. If your partner could go back in time, what would they change?

_____

8. Has your partner ever broken the law (aside from traffic violations)?

Yes   No

9. What is the weirdest experience of your partner's life?

_____

_____

_____

10. When has your partner been most scared?

_____

_____

_____

11. How many times did your partner move houses before the age of eighteen?

_____

12. What's your partner's favorite date with you?

_____

_____

_____

13. When was the first time your partner flew on a plane?

_____

14. At what age did your partner leave the home they grew up in?

_____

15. My partner's worst job ever was . . .

_____

16. How old was your partner when they first voted?

_____

17. Has your partner ever been fired from a job?

    Yes   No

18. Has your partner ever won a contest before?

    Yes   No

If yes, what was the prize?

_____

19. What was your partner's first car?

_____

20. Which languages are your partner fluent in?

_____

21. What was your partner's first impression of you?

_____

_____

_____

22. Your partner's favorite memory with you is . . .

_____

_____

_____

You are done with yours. Turn the page to review your quiz results together.

Review Your Results

Discuss both of your answers and review how you and your partner view things differently.

Use this review as a chance to revisit any question(s) you would like to have a deeper conversation about with your partner.

Quiz Results for this Section

What's the total number of questions you got correct about your partner?

Partner A: _____

Partner B: _____

The partner with the highest score gets to be surprised by the partner with the lowest score. Flowers? A day trip? Their favorite people over for dinner? A relaxing day at the spa?

If it's a tie, reminisce about your love story together.

Quiz 7
Dreaming Ahead

(Partner A: It's your turn to answer.)

1. Name one thing on your partner's bucket list.

_____

2. Name a country your partner would love to visit.

_____

3. What is a goal your partner and you have in common?

_____

4. What's your partner's dream vacation?

_____

5. What's the one thing your partner wants to change in their life right now?

_____

6. If your partner could become fluent in another language, what would it be?

_____

7. What is your partner's ultimate life dream?

_____

_____

_____

8. What does your partner believe the meaning of life is?

_____

_____

_____

9. If your partner could do one of the following, which would they choose?

a. Go to a rooftop party in a big city   b. Go to a five-star restaurant

c. Have a deep conversation about life   d. Sit outside, enjoying a good book by the fire

e. Hike a challenging mountain   f. Go to a concert

g. Go to a sporting event

Awesome, you just finished yours. Now, turn the page for your partner to complete theirs.

Dreaming Ahead

*(Partner **B**: It's your turn to answer.)*

1. Name one thing on your partner's bucket list.

_____

2. Name a country your partner would love to visit.

_____

3. What is a goal your partner and you have in common?

_____

4. What's your partner's dream vacation?

_____

5. What's the one thing your partner wants to change in their life right now?

_____

6. If your partner could become fluent in another language, what would it be?

_____

7. What is your partner's ultimate life dream?

_____

_____

_____

8. What does your partner believe the meaning of life is?

_____

_____

_____

9. If your partner could do one of the following, which would they choose?

a. Go to a rooftop party in a big city   b. Go to a five-star restaurant

c. Have a deep conversation about life   d. Sit outside, enjoying a good book by the fire

e. Hike a challenging mountain   f. Go to a concert

g. Go to a sporting event

You are done with yours. Turn the page to review your quiz results together.

Review Your Results

Discuss both of your answers and review how you and your partner view things differently.

Use this review as a chance to revisit any question(s) you would like to have a deeper conversation about with your partner.

Quiz Results for this Section

What's the total number of questions you got correct about your partner?

Partner A: _____

Partner B: _____

The partner with the highest score gets to pick the destination of your next date.

If it's a tie, have a conversation about your next vacation or getaway.

Quiz 8
This or That

(Partner A: It's your turn to answer.)

Circle what your partner prefers:

1. Big party or small gathering?
2. Dine out or delivery?
3. Laundry or dishes?
4. Forest or beach?
5. Desert or mountains?
6. Sunrise or sunset?
7. Train or plane?
8. City or countryside?
9. Beer or wine?
10. Passenger or driver?
11. Time or money?
12. Bacon or kale?
13. Online or in-store shopping?
14. Card game or board game?
15. Clean the bathroom or clean the kitchen?
16. Massage or bubble bath with candles?
17. Skydiving or bungee jumping?
18. Morning sex or breakfast in bed?
19. Coffee or tea?
20. Burial or cremation?

Awesome, you just finished yours. Now, turn the page for your partner to complete theirs.

This or That

*(Partner **B**: It's your turn to answer.)*

Circle what your partner prefers:

1. Big party or small gathering?
2. Dine out or delivery?
3. Laundry or dishes?
4. Forest or beach?
5. Desert or mountains?
6. Sunrise or sunset?
7. Train or plane?
8. City or countryside?
9. Beer or wine?
10. Passenger or driver?
11. Time or money?
12. Bacon or kale?
13. Online or in-store shopping?
14. Card game or board game?
15. Clean the bathroom or clean the kitchen?
16. Massage or bubble bath with candles?
17. Skydiving or bungee jumping?
18. Morning sex or breakfast in bed?
19. Coffee or tea?
20. Burial or cremation?

You are done with yours. Turn the page to review your quiz results together.

Review Your Results

Discuss both of your answers and review how you and your partner view things differently.

Use this review as a chance to revisit any question(s) you would like to have a deeper conversation about with your partner.

Quiz Results for this Section

What's the total number of questions you got correct about your partner?

Partner A: _____

Partner B: _____

The partner with the highest score gets to sign you both up for a class they've wanted to take with their partner.

If it's a tie, cook a meal together.

Quiz 9
Would Your Partner Rather

(Partner A: It's your turn to answer.)

Circle what your partner would prefer to do.

1. Lose their sense of smell or lose their sense of taste?

2. Cuddle in the morning or cuddle at night?

3. Spend time by the lake or spend time by the ocean?

4. Get up early or stay up late?

5. Spend the day inside or spend the day outside?

6. Have breakfast in bed or a candlelit dinner?

7. Dance under the moon or dance in a club?

8. Go on a road trip or fly to a destination?

9. Lose the ability to see or lose the ability to walk?

10. Live in a place where it is always hot or live in a place where it is always cold?

11. Be deaf or be blind?

12. Get matching piercings or get matching tattoos?

13. Cook together or bake together?

14. Cuddle by a fireplace or cuddle beside a window overlooking the ocean?

15. Read a book together or watch a TV show together?

Awesome, you just finished yours. Now, turn the page for your partner to complete theirs.

Would Your Partner Rather

*(Partner **B**: It's your turn to answer.)*

Circle what your partner would prefer to do.

1. Lose their sense of smell or lose their sense of taste?

2. Cuddle in the morning or cuddle at night?

3. Spend time by the lake or spend time by the ocean?

4. Get up early or stay up late?

5. Spend the day inside or spend the day outside?

6. Have breakfast in bed or a candlelit dinner?

7. Dance under the moon or dance in a club?

8. Go on a road trip or fly to a destination?

9. Lose the ability to see or lose the ability to walk?

10. Live in a place where it is always hot or live in a place where it is always cold?

11. Be deaf or be blind?

12. Get matching piercings or get matching tattoos?

13. Cook together or bake together?

14. Cuddle by a fireplace or cuddle beside a window overlooking the ocean?

15. Read a book together or watch a TV show together?

You are done with yours. Turn the page to review your quiz results together.

Review Your Results

Discuss both of your answers and review how you and your partner view things differently.

Use this review as a chance to revisit any question(s) you would like to have a deeper conversation about with your partner.

Quiz Results for this Section

What's the total number of questions you got correct about your partner?

Partner A: _____

Partner B: _____

The partner with the highest score gets a full-body massage from the partner with the lowest score.

If it's a tie, put on your favorite music and dance together.

Quiz 10
Ultimate Fantasy

*(Partner **A**: It's your turn to answer.)*

1. During sex, your partner enjoys . . .

    a. Being in control   b. Taking turns   c. You being in control

2. Circle which one your partner prefers:

a. Slow sex or rough sex or a mixture of both

b. Being on top or being on the bottom?

c. Being kinky or being romantic

d. Sex with the lights on or sex with the lights off?

e. Receiving oral or giving oral or both?

f. Sex with music on or having sex with music off?

g. To have you screaming and moaning during sex or being quiet?

3. What's your partner's favorite sex position?

_____

4. Does your partner like dirty talk during sex?

    Yes   No.

5. Ideally, how long does your partner like foreplay to last?

    a. Less than ten minutes   b. Eleven to twenty minutes

    c. More than twenty-one minutes

6. Your partner's favorite sex toys are:

_____

7. Which sex toy would your partner like to try?

_____

8. Does your partner like to be woken up with sex or oral sex by you?

    Yes   No

9. Would your partner be interested in roleplay and costumes?

    Yes   No

10. Does your partner enjoy receiving oral sex?

    Yes   No

11. Does your partner enjoy giving oral sex?

    Yes   No

12. During sex, does your partner like to:

a. Be spanked?	Yes	No
b. Be tied up?	Yes	No
c. Be blindfolded?	Yes	No
d. Experience sensory deprivation?	Yes	No
e. Play games?	Yes	No
f. Be consensual non-consensual?	Yes	No
g. Be called names?	Yes	No
h. Use sex toys?	Yes	No
i. Be choked?	Yes	No

Awesome, you just finished yours. Now, turn the page for your partner to complete theirs.

Ultimate Fantasy

*(Partner **B**: It's your turn to answer.)*

1. During sex, your partner enjoys . . .

    a. Being in control   b. Taking turns   c. You being in control

2. Circle which one your partner prefers:

a. Slow sex or rough sex or a mixture of both

b. Being on top or being on the bottom?

c. Being kinky or being romantic

d. Sex with the lights on or sex with the lights off?

e. Receiving oral or giving oral or both?

f. Sex with music on or having sex with music off?

g. To have you screaming and moaning during sex or being quiet?

3. What's your partner's favorite sex position?

_____

4. Does your partner like dirty talk during sex?

     Yes   No.

5. Ideally, how long does your partner like foreplay to last?

     a. Less than ten minutes   b. Eleven to twenty minutes

     c. More than twenty-one minutes

6. Your partner's favorite sex toys are:

_____

7. Which sex toy would your partner like to try?

_____

8. Does your partner like to be woken up with sex or oral sex by you?

     Yes   No

9. Would your partner be interested in roleplay and costumes?

     Yes   No

10. Does your partner enjoy receiving oral sex?

     Yes   No

11. Does your partner enjoy giving oral sex?

     Yes   No

12. During sex, does your partner like to:

a. Be spanked?	Yes	No
b. Be tied up?	Yes	No
c. Be blindfolded?	Yes	No
d. Experience sensory deprivation?	Yes	No
e. Play games?	Yes	No
f. Be consensual non-consensual?	Yes	No
g. Be called names?	Yes	No
h. Use sex toys?	Yes	No
i. Be choked?	Yes	No

You are done with yours. Turn the page to review your quiz results together.

Review Your Results

Discuss both of your answers and review how you and your partner view things differently.

Use this review as a chance to revisit any question(s) you would like to have a deeper conversation about with your partner.

Quiz Results for this Section

What's the total number of questions you got correct about your partner?

Partner A: _____

Partner B: _____

The partner with the highest score gets to have one of their fantasies come true.

If it's a tie, talk about why you want to experience one of your sexual fantasies.

Quiz 11
Bedroom Magic

(Partner A: It's your turn to answer.)

1. Your partner has a sex drive that is:

    a. High   b. Average   c. Low

2. Does your partner enjoy sex with you?

    Yes   No

3. Does your partner use sex as a:

    a. Way of connecting with you   b. Physical release

    c. Other: _____

4. Your partner's favorite part of sex with you is . . .

_____

5. What are your partner's top three sexual fantasies?

a. _____

b. _____

c _____

6. What would your partner say is the sexiest thing you have done for them?

_____

7. What's their number-one sexual turn-on?

_____

8. What's their number-one sexual turn-off?

_____

9. What's their favorite time of day to have sex?

a. Morning   b. Afternoon   c. Evening   d. Night

10. What is one thing your partner loves to do after a session of love-making?

a. Kissing   b. Pillow talk   c. Sleep   d. Cuddling

11. About how long does it take for your partner to be aroused again for another session of lovemaking?

_____

12. The best way to flirt with your partner is . . .

_____

13. Your partner would say the best sex you have had together to date is . . .

_____

14. What does your partner love about your sex life?

_____

15. What's the riskiest place you've had sex with your partner?

_____

16. Is your partner satisfied with your sex life?

Yes   No

17. During sex, your partner orgasms:

a. Frequently   b. Sometimes   c. Rarely   d. Never

18. What does your partner believe is the biggest obstacle to your sex life?

_____

19. How would your partner rate your sex life on a scale of one to ten, ten being the best?

    1   2   3   4   5   6   7   8   9   10

20. Does your partner feel comfortable talking about your sex life, or discussing sexual needs/wants/issues that arise?

    Yes   No   Most of the time

21. Your partner initiates sex the most in your relationship.

    a. True   b. False

Awesome, you just finished yours. Now, turn the page for your partner to complete theirs.

Bedroom Magic

*(Partner **B**: It's your turn to answer.)*

1. Your partner has a sex drive that is:

   a. High   b. Average   c. Low

2. Does your partner enjoy sex with you?

   Yes   No

3. Does your partner use sex as a:

   a. Way of connecting with you   b. Physical release

   c. Other: _____

4. Your partner's favorite part of sex with you is . . .

_____

5. What are your partner's top three sexual fantasies?

a. _____

b. _____

c _____

6. What would your partner say is the sexiest thing you have done for them?

_____

7. What's their number-one sexual turn-on?

_____

8. What's their number-one sexual turn-off?

_____

9. What's their favorite time of day to have sex?

      a. Morning   b. Afternoon   c. Evening   d. Night

10. What is one thing your partner loves to do after a session of love-making?

      a. Kissing   b. Pillow talk   c. Sleep   d. Cuddling

11. About how long does it take for your partner to be aroused again for another session of lovemaking?

_____

12. The best way to flirt with your partner is . . .

_____

13. Your partner would say the best sex you have had together to date is . . .

_____

14. What does your partner love about your sex life?

_____

15. What's the riskiest place you've had sex with your partner?

_____

16. Is your partner satisfied with your sex life?

     Yes   No

17. During sex, your partner orgasms:

     a. Frequently   b. Sometimes   c. Rarely   d. Never

18. What does your partner believe is the biggest obstacle to your sex life?

_____

19. How would your partner rate your sex life on a scale of one to ten, ten being the best?

     1   2   3   4   5   6   7   8   9   10

20. Does your partner feel comfortable talking about your sex life, or discussing sexual needs/wants/issues that arise?

      Yes   No   Most of the time

21. Your partner initiates sex the most in your relationship.

      a. True   b. False

You are done with yours. Turn the page to review your quiz results together.

Review Your Results

Discuss both of your answers and review how you and your partner view things differently.

Use this review as a chance to revisit any question(s) you would like to have a deeper conversation about with your partner.

Quiz Results for this Section

What's the total number of questions you got correct about your partner?

Partner A: _____

Partner B: _____

The partner with the highest score gets a sexy gift bought by their partner.

If it's a tie, have fun exploring each other's bodies.

Quiz 12
Relationship Checkup

(Partner A: It's your turn to answer.)

1. What is something you want your partner to know about how you feel about them?

_____

_____

_____

_____

_____

2. What are five things you are grateful for about your partner?

_____

_____

_____

_____

_____

3. On a scale of one to ten, with 10 being the highest, how would you rate your relationship with your partner?

Fun:	1	2	3	4	5	6	7	8	9	10
Friendship:	1	2	3	4	5	6	7	8	9	10
Quality time:	1	2	3	4	5	6	7	8	9	10
Romance:	1	2	3	4	5	6	7	8	9	10
Emotional intimacy:	1	2	3	4	5	6	7	8	9	10
Communication:	1	2	3	4	5	6	7	8	9	10
Physical intimacy:	1	2	3	4	5	6	7	8	9	10

4. What could you both do to make each category a little better?

Fun:

_____

_____

_____

Friendship:

_____

_____

_____

Quality time:

_____

_____

_____

Romance:

_____

_____

_____

Emotional intimacy:

_____

_____

_____

Communication:

_____

_____

_____

Physical intimacy:

_____

_____

_____

5. What is one thing you believe your partner could work on to help make them better?

_____

_____

_____

6. What is one thing your partner would say your relationship is lacking?

_____

_____

_____

7. What is one romantic gesture you will do for your partner next week?

_____

_____

_____

Awesome, you just finished yours. Now, turn the page for your partner to complete theirs.

Relationship Checkup

*(Partner **B**: It's your turn to answer.)*

1. What is something you want your partner to know about how you feel about them?

_____

_____

_____

_____

_____

2. What are five things you are grateful for about your partner?

_____

_____

_____

_____

_____

3. On a scale of one to ten, with 10 being the highest, how would you rate your relationship with your partner?

Fun:	1	2	3	4	5	6	7	8	9	10
Friendship:	1	2	3	4	5	6	7	8	9	10
Quality time:	1	2	3	4	5	6	7	8	9	10
Romance:	1	2	3	4	5	6	7	8	9	10
Emotional intimacy:	1	2	3	4	5	6	7	8	9	10
Communication:	1	2	3	4	5	6	7	8	9	10
Physical intimacy:	1	2	3	4	5	6	7	8	9	10

4. What could you both do to make each category a little better?

Fun:

_____

_____

_____

Friendship:

_____

_____

_____

Quality time:

_____

_____

_____

Romance:

_____

_____

_____

Emotional intimacy:

_____

_____

_____

Communication:

_____

_____

_____

Physical intimacy:

_____

_____

_____

5. What is one thing you believe your partner could work on to help make them better?

_____

_____

_____

6. What is one thing your partner would say your relationship is lacking?

_____

_____

_____

7. What is one romantic gesture you will do for your partner next week?

_____

_____

_____

You are done with yours. Turn the page to review your quiz results together.

Review Your Relationship

You're a couple so when you win, you win together, and the same goes for losing.

First, discuss your answers to see how you both feel about where you are in your relationship. Use this review as a chance to revisit any question(s) you would like to have a deeper conversation about with your partner.

Second, come up with a plan to improve the areas that need strengthening, one at a time so you don't get overwhelmed. Talk about your relationship and discuss what you can do to make it better, stronger, and more fulfilling

Finally, take some time to work on making your relationship even better and create a list of goals for your relationship. Don't forget to check in from time to time with each other and see the progress you've made as well as continuing to enhance other areas of your relationship.

To discover more fun, insightful, and free quizzes for couples visit:

www.ourpeacefulfamily.com/funquizzes

Thank you

Congratulations on completing this quiz book! We hope this book has opened up some dialogue and strengthened your relationship with your partner.

If you enjoyed using this book, please leave us a review on Amazon and share the book with other couples. You can even gift this book to your friends and family.

To receive email updates about future books, courses, and more, visit our website below to join our book fan community today:

www.ourpeacefulfamily.com/bookfan

Thank you again for choosing and using our book!

Marcus and Ashley Kusi

Enjoy your marriage; enjoy your life.

Other Books by Marcus and Ashley

Our Bucket List Adventures: A Journal for Couples

Our Love Story Journal: 138 Questions and Prompts for Couples to Complete Together

Questions for Couples: 469 Thought-Provoking Conversation Starters for Connecting, Building Trust, and Rekindling Intimacy

Our Gratitude Journal: 52 Weeks of Love, Mindfulness, and Appreciation for Couples

Emotional and Sexual Intimacy in Marriage: How to Connect or Reconnect With Your Spouse, Grow Together, and Strengthen Your Marriage

Communication in Marriage: How to Communicate with Your Spouse Without Fighting

First Year of Marriage: The Newlywed's Guide to Building a Strong Foundation and Adjusting to Married Life

About the Authors

Marcus and Ashley help overwhelmed newlyweds adjust to married life, and inspire married couples to improve their marriage so they can become better husbands and wives.

They do this by using their own marriage experience, gleaning wisdom from other married couples, and sharing what works for them through their website and marriage podcast, *The First Year Marriage Show*.

Visit the website below to listen to their podcast.

www.firstyearmarriage.com

To learn more about them, visit:

www.ourpeacefulfamily.com

Marriage is a lifelong journey that thrives on love, commitment, trust, respect, communication, patience, and companionship.

—Ashley and Marcus Kusi

Made in the USA
San Bernardino, CA
07 January 2020